# CHRONIC

～

# CHRONIC

❦

## D. A. Powell

**Graywolf Press**
Saint Paul, Minnesota

Publication of this volume is made possible in part by a grant provided by the Minnesota State Arts
Board, through an appropriation by the Minnesota State Legislature; a grant from the Wells Fargo Foun-
dation Minnesota; and a grant from the National Endowment for the Arts, which believes that a great
nation deserves great art. Significant support has also been provided by the Bush Foundation; Target; the
McKnight Foundation; and other generous contributions from foundations, corporations, and individu-
als. To these organizations and individuals we offer our heartfelt thanks.

Published by Graywolf Press

2402 University Avenue, Suite 203

Saint Paul, Minnesota 55114

www.graywolfpress.org

Published in the United States of America

ISBN 978-1-55597-516-6

2  4  6  8  9  7  5  3  1

First Graywolf Printing, 2009

Library of Congress Control Number: 2008935598

Cover design: Kyle G. Hunter
Cover photo: J. Henry Fair

*for*
*Haines Eason*

*after all*

# CHRONIC

## Initial C

## Chronic

## Terminal C

Time robs us of all, even of memory: oft as a boy I recall
that with song I would lay the long summer days to
rest. Now I have forgotten all my songs.
—Virgil, *Eclogue IX*

# CHRONIC

&

# Initial C

~

# no picnic

plain cloth cast upon the cool banks, the mere warbling frogs

        an interrupted repast, uninterrupted pile of leavings

the parallax of bodies which are and are not ours

        uncomfortable shift, uncomfortable shuffle

so many of the best days seem minor forms of nearness
        that easily fall among the dropseed:  a rind, a left-behind


I watched the bluejays provoke each other, eager to scrap

        if I could make the world my own and be satisfied
I'd say that you did not see them, nor hear their anxious fuss
        but you were watching.   I, in fact, was not


        forget that hour of meanness.   we should not have been
perched on the vestige of evening, treading that same gunny cloth

## california poppy

shuddering back to this coastline, craggy old goat rock
or the sweep of dune where judah meets squid-ink pacific
no more the nomad for now.   or—stubbornly—everywhere, as each
exotic dancer filling the cracked sidewalks of north beach

as the indigent waving his tattered placard on the island
[what we call this meridian near church & dolores where the fronds
of palmtrees are stippled with shrill green or yellow lorikeets]
saying "come to my island:  live cast-off cargo on this desolate reef"

—as the transmissible fruitfly larvae ravaging local oranges
as a fragile head upon a thinning stalk that somehow manages
to clasp hands at evening and send up its muttering entreaty
so small you might not notice, so ubiquitous, you see

so many ugly little flapping faces pocking city car lots,
the freeway onramps, the piss-scented flowerpots,
the unclaimed and untended plots (so few—and yet they're dense
with the wispy strands of hair and the folds of sallow tents)

that you've your right to ignore them, to ignore the grasping
fingers and bloated waxy face of the wildly surviving thing
that once was somebody's boutonnière, somebody's flash of light,
trail of phosphorescent streetlamps punctuating the homeless night

# central valley

earlier the curtain of smoke hung as dark spots on pecked fruit
plumes still rising over paddies where the rice straw smoldered

kids like me blowing black snot into sleeves and checked bandannas
the farmers—almost extinct— wheezing along the earthen dikes
and the sky a mass of black lung:  spittle settling upon the nutsedge

terrible immanence of spring:  among the tules, marsh wrens trilled
& bitterns stalled vertically against the edge of irrigation ponds
where crawdads haggled a mouse, its carcass scavenged into bits

unstoppable noise from the slough:  suckwhistle and croak of kites
the honk of canada geese not unlike the child's complaint of croup

couldn't describe the smell of almond wood, I know:  couldn't describe
that marriage between bitter sod and brief light of joss paper burning

here I inhaled first plum blossoms and took the yellowjacket stings
saying "sticks, I live in the sticks, don't drive me home I'll sleep instead
on your rug, be your boy, just ask me to spread my legs, I'll spread"

my mind's a dingy billow of slashed stalk combusting in the slade
it opens like a gopher hole inopportune.   opens its sorry leafage
against the buttes, against the blooms, against each new season

and a crazy man who ignited his shed and home:  his laugh
a kind of coughing laugh:  or the cry of a common hawk

# crematorium at sierra view cemetery next to the high school

impoverished graveyard:  mangy green triangle where two freeways form a crotch

twenty yards from the gym and the AG shop:  see, it's morty's mom's funeral today
there's morty in a tie, his dad's head rocking:  the pendulum of a clock tsk-tsks

holes just the size of flowerbeds claim sleek boxes.    marry me, you ruined seed

all semester they open and gnash their yellowy teeth:  *there goes mike,* we say—
his hearse lumbering through the iron gate—remember:  he used to drive so fast

and then that smokestack poking its head above the surrounding grass

so that others—ever mindful of space, perhaps—could singe and shrivel on oven racks
blazing into eggshell-colored ash collected in old penny jars and in paper sacks

*there goes dusty* [pointing at the belching puffs that tumbled over the valley]

between PE and molecular biology the smoke you'd sneak:  half tobacco, half human
white alloy of the usual carcinogens and damon pettibone's granny.    or a bit of mike

that chest that—before it caved against the steering wheel—felt strong and sinewy

## on the tarmac

fatigued you guarded the electric fence, which guarded the planes
        which guarded the covert america—that guarded place

you coveted the steel fuselage, the ticking of the engine's prop
        and longed to scrooch inside, to know the gyroscope

push forward on the stick, bank, and feel the centrifugal pull
        as the ailerons tip, deflect and lift you into pressured roll


therefore the escalating sun, the takeoff into swipe of frigatebirds
        choppy course, your wind-bruted blue momentum, turn


the buzz—you could not say coordinates, your next approach
        that shifted from visual to instruments—was cordoned off

evasive action—may day concede you to the crackling wire
        those hoarse clearings, a pitch that seemed to thwart the air

# early havoc

didn't buy me no taps for no shoes, didn't dance
ballroom or otherwise, got no piano lessons
nor elocution (as probably you can guess) nor voice

in the methodist pageant there was one line I spoke:
"lo, I bring you tidings of great joy, for unto you this day
and I forget the rest — uneasy relationship with christ:

as if he were a mutt and I was a boy — which I was —
and more than a few times the boy had been bit
the dog had been pelted with driveway gravel, and so

we regarded each other with . . . that was *the zoo story*
I caught myself just on the verge of stealing a line from —
later, during what I should call the showbiz period:

"I am the ghost of christmas past," I say.   long past?
your past.   [something]   scrooge: "I am much obliged
for rousing me in the dead of night to discuss my welfare

then the burning of atlanta, followed quickly by
the burning of hollywood:  that's *the day of the locust*
everybody on fire, karen black, like me, & desperate to be

## clutch and pumps

*if I were in your shoes,* you purse your mouth
but you were never in my shoes, chinaberry
nor I in yours:  the cherry ash of fags
burns your path down the scatty streets

your smile wraps round *pumps* with a smack
the jawbone of a mighty red croc
who served up his behind to your toes
jagged bite marks:  the hem of your frock

tombs, sister, you've got lithic tombs for hips
one chimney stack where a bbq pit should be
you say that I'm in janitor drag this year:  as last
*do these tits go with these shoulders?*  why ask me?

those talons you cultivate I do admire
the cochineal cheeks the flirty lashes
*I don't want to live in a clutch purse town*
you snap:  and yet everything matches

# coronation fanfare [in the style of edith sitwell]

liturgical hibiscus loves to wear surgical gloves
into bed on safari with heinrich the elephant boy

her salad days are moulting:  unbolting the cabinet door
as one upon whom reproach seems superfluous brooche

she *te deums* with tedium shucking her mitre-filled nightie
for acolytes heinrich and huck [heinrich's coptic double]

industrious heinrich arises at crackling noon
re-entering the room with surprises of beans and toast

sweetmeats and barium ooze from her fistula
cystic hibiscus—with plaster and spatula—

arranges her face:  ascending a throne

# come live with me and be my love

lately in the sanitarium, locked up with you, dishabille
beneath a ceiling of achromatic tubes, the bald glare
of a day room large and dumb, seeming distant as the hills

surrounded by loons, and orderlies with pinned-back hair
I have sought your degenerate company, incandescent
even in the corner where you are (you *are* in that wheelchair)


or am I the one who's no more dear, fumbling convalescent
while you take the stage like a salvage scow:  steal my number
draw me limping by rote into this dramatic duet, this moment

reorganizing our folding card tables, folding chairs, somber
face of the charge nurse, the dixie cups with measured pills —
one of us will be discharged soon.    for now, let's act like lovers

## cul-de-sac

so you're momentarily enchanted, and so the gables—
        like bayonets—point to jet trails overhead

just when you think you've arrived, you have nothing
            except fido:  good old fido
who frisks against your calf and plays dead in the carport

or maybe you have your 2.3 kids, if your tubes aren't tied—
            and why haven't your tubes been tied?

legacy of spittle and legacy of snot:  fat emeralds, little gems
                a fiefdom in the alveoli at the end of congested trachea
where, home again from the desert, you might sleepwalk
            in a ratty housecoat and a pair of standard-issue clogs

where your flagpole shivers above the mailbox
            and the postman, in his jeep, cheerfully avoids you


                            toys in the yard, little boys:
you must not mourn the next year or the next

# lipsync [with a nod to lipps, inc.]

put your mouth around a juicy candy, coat
with red dye no.  2: *pucker, fucker.*    then blow

out the candles on the cake:  that's how
you make believe you're holding a trembling c note

the *la la la* is like licking pussy  [see note]

> — note:    that night I fell into a pile with incandescent
> bodies, an ocean of womyn lapping the rocks
> said:  come down here and be our playtoy
>
> did.    and diddled.  [or *dawdled?*]  as in PLAYBOY
> I slid up into the one who straddled me.    shaved box
> the warm folds of her felt as a man's stubbly chin
>
> my tongue went into dark places, as a moray eel slips
> *funkytown* on the hi-fi, I mouthed the lyrics
>
> > *take me, won't you take me*
> > *take me, won't you take me, &c.—*

what phrase lingers in the back of your larynx
snookums, you could swallow me in three gulps:  be so assured

if you don't know the tune, mumble *watermelon, hummingbird*
gesture grandly the way you squirmed between my lips

# cosmos, late blooming

already the warm days taper to a plumate end:  sky, where is your featherbed
some portion for me to fall to, in my contused and stricken state
not the extravagant robe I bartered for:  tatters, pinked edges, unpressed

lord, I'm a homely child, scrabbling in the midden for my keep
why should you send this strapping gardener, hay in his teeth, to tend me
now that the showy crown begins to dip like a paper saucer

surely he'll not content with corrupted flesh that dismantles daily
so singular this closing act:  spectacular ruin, the spark that descends in air
might he find no thrill in this trodden bower.   ragamuffin sum of veins

in my mouth the mausoleum of refusal:  everything died inside me
including fish and vegetables, language and lovers, desire, yes, and passion
how could I make room in this crypt for another sorrow:  caretaker:

lost man, these brambles part for your boots, denizened to my lot
your hand upon my stem now grasps the last shoots of summer
choose me for your chaplet, sweetheart.   wasted were my early flowers

# sprig of lilac

in a week you could watch me crumble to smut:  spent hues
spent perfumes.    dust upon the lapel where a moment I rested

yes, the moths have visited and deposited their velvet egg mass
the gnats were here:  they smelled the wilt and blight.    they salivated

in the folds of my garments:  you could practically taste the rot

look at the pluck you've made of my heart:  it broke open in your hands
oddments of ravished leaves:  blossom blast and dieback:  petals drooping

we kissed briefly in the deathless spring.    the koi pond hummed with flies

unbutton me now from your grasp.    no, hold tighter, let me disappear
into your nostrils, into your skin, a powdery smudge against your rough cheek

## continental divide

had no direction to go but up:  and this, the shattery road
its surface graining,  trickle in late thaw—is nothing amiss?
—*this melt*, the sign assures us, *natural cycle*
> and *whoosh,* the water a dream of forgotten white

past aspens colored in sulfur, they trembled, would
—poor sinners in redemption song—shed their tainted leaves

I tell you what boy I was, writing lyrics to reflect my passions:
the smell of a bare neck in summer
a thin trail of hairs disappearing below the top button of cut-offs
the lean, arched back of a cyclist straining to ascend a hill

in the starlight I wandered:  streets no better than fields
the cul-de-sacs of suburbia just as treacherous, just as empty

if wood doves sang in the branches of the acacias, I could not hear them
anyone lost in that same night was lost in another tract

the air pulsed and dandelion pollen blew from green stalks
> —that was all

and yes, someone took me in his car.    and another against the low fence
in the park at the end of our block.    under the willow branches
where gnats made a furious cloud at dawn and chased us away

I knew how it felt to lie in a patch of marigolds:  golden stains
the way morning swarmed a hidden rooftop, the catbirds singing
the feel of ruin upon lips rubbed raw throughout the night


granite peaks:  here, the earth has asserted itself.  and the ice asserted
and human intimacies conspired to keep us low and apart

for an ice age I knew you only as an idea of longing:
a voice in the next yard, whispering through the chink
a vagabond outlined against the sky, among the drying grass


we journey this day to darkness:  the chasm walls lift us on their scaly backs
the glaciers relinquish their secrets:  that sound is the ice bowing
and the sound underneath, the trickle:  the past released, disappearing


you pinnacle of my life, stand with me on this brink
half-clouded basin caked in flat grays, the very demise of green

you have surmounted the craggy boundary between us


you open the earth for me, receiving these amber last leaves

# gospel on the dial, with intermittent static

that bough, emissary of shade, held off the rain we quivered under

igneous rubble broke tumulting creek water into rolling sugar boil

& *thou deliverest*, station on the wireless, lights blinking from sutro tower


inside the sequoia's bison bark, its jagged and cracked skin jolted open
cleft labia by lightning torn into a wooden vault the size of two

me plus you:  an old god saved us from the wrack of this january rain
himself a wayfaring stag trodding the lichen of these prehistoric woods


sometimes I prayed to be plowed under in some ordinary field
a blue slink pod or a patch of miner's lettuce to mark my forehead

no lifetime should bear such silence as these past few years have offered:
canned soup, old library books, drafty rooms and empty pill bottles

seizure, I said, blunt force trauma to the head.   anything but the alone
that creeps up the wall like mildew until one must face the fact of it

that tree that penetration and erosion— history and irresponsible lovers'
carved names— withstood: cracked cathedral spire with its dumb notes

echoing the lonely spotted owl: how long to linger in the cavity of this trunk
its song familiar to us, the scent of burnt resin returning from beyond

## that night in the foxhole with the pfc

my battles are not the same as yours.    this tired army
ghosts me into marble, outstretching veins of rocket trails
another dead soldier under a chunk of monument stone

tonight I'm a messkit, you snore, you bore into me, swiss army
each twitch of your gadgetbox, horning to destroy my sleep

pressed ration, I stir thick in my own twisted dream

don't enter this bivouac where I rustle:  in camouflage leaves
I'm covered and a whiff of the onslaught is coming:
the fall that radios its turbid breath, advancing, dusky wood

so many caresses I'd allow you but [  ]
assist you in taking my flank except [  ]
straddle your bare legs in an arc of shrapnel yet [  ]

[footfalls:    now leaves him]      sc. ii:  advancing to sack another city
                                 trumpet turn and missile flare:  I have no air
rush?    just the slope of breathing figures in this scalled landscape

oh atomic god:  withered are the young tonight.    keep my buddy safe
under, and not upon, his shield.    tear down the maps in the infirmary
as some stranger hand moves in to stifle a kid's unbearable song

## coit tower & us

breeze up through the covert tiers and foliate terraces
a skewing of white jasmine stars, stammering bamboo

sedulous we ascend through the maze of concrete steps
conglomerate paths and sideyards scattered in terra cotta

collars turned against the evening news telegraphing
through weak-stemmed mallow and firethorn shrubs


we cleave the path as a form of music:  long notes
quavering low through our bodies the way the foghorn sings
repeats its mumbled history against the fluted tower
this stone column the girth of a nozzle:  monument to rescue


                    [interlude: 1906]
*faultline slippage and infirm topography:  havoc of granite balustrades*
*beams that plunged earthward and plaster that lurched on cross-walls*
*tumbling brick and rock.    then the lick of flames against the sky*

*soot-smudged faces and oily biceps carrying hoses or in bucket brigades*
*as the poorly clad and scorched streamed down the peninsula*


some nights I feel that loss as if my own trembling musculature
lies concealed under a rubbled city, listening to the mission bells

you pull me from this collapsed architecture, you too a kind of pillar
you almost have that same heft, as we climb, I see you stronger

past all these houses that pebble the hill in a kind of cairn
and at the apex, this marker.    and from the marker, a prospect
white sails dappling the gray waves beyond the swaying bridge
*this is what the infinite feels like,* you say, take my tentative hand

## meditating upon the meaning of the line "clams on the halfshell and rollerskates" in the song *good times* by chic

even the business of dying must be set aside occasionally.   glaucous-winged gulls drafting
the last ferry across the bay:  lights of the city growing more luminous, more inviting

who could have guessed love's a palpable thing:  a dark splotch of kelp in the shoals
or a mountain lion that prowls the edge of UC's cypress woods:  desires a young student
ivory mandible slack and slavering.   at the amber hour snarls its empty bowels

touch:  that sensation I'd almost lost.   or how to curl into another body hermit-crab style
the grouchy old man in my mirror said "bare terror."   said "who's sharing your towels?"

go away, you bitter cuss.   it's still 1980 somewhere, some corner of your dark apartment
where the mystery of the lyric hasn't faded.   and love is in the chorus waiting to be born

## the half-forgotten voice of yma sumac

hushed the botanical garden's inca princess, muted horn
with a blush of apricot swathing her welcome kisser

absent the monarchy and not wistful, waiting at the gate
not in the cloudforest, missing the crooked mountain road,—

her guttural her clement her piping voice:  her trailing bellchime
straggles a bezzled kingdom:  steep cliffs, tangle of difficult vines

all the buzzing flies and the nickering wrens amass

a chatter monkey, small-boned and rusty, chews his fleas

her majesty declines.    some other sound wastes the air—tonight

if I should hear her moving through the brugmansia trees
who could blame me for the way my head, formerly stalwart, bends

for a white-haired man sits under the trumpet flowers
where the universe used to burnish its darkened edge

# [not the musical:] south pacific

sailing into exile:  a doubt-filled sailor—yawing, tacking
waves scrape the sky in all directions

great bowl of ocean and no land in sight
my schooner lists:  threatens to keel

mutinous crew setting me adrift
in that damnable life raft

they'll fly skull and crossbones now:  they'll take
hardtack and grog while I thirst against the equator


pollux, could that be you above the brume?
away, my reflection, my little lack of faith

## confessions of a teenage drama queen

I was a male war bride.    I was a spy
so I married an axe murderer.    I married joan
I married a monster from outer space

I am guilty, I am the cheese, I am a fugitive from a chain gang
maybe I'll come home in the spring.    I'll cry tomorrow
whose life is it anyway?    it's a wonderful life

I want to live.    I want someone to eat cheese with
who am I this time?    I am cuba.    I am a sex addict
why was I born?    why must I die?    I could go on singing

I'll sleep when I'm dead.    I know who killed me
I was nineteen, I was a teenage werewolf, just kill me
kiss me, kill me.    kill me later.    kill me again

give me a sailor, if I had my way, I'd rather be rich
I wouldn't be in your shoes.    I wish I had wings
I wish I were in dixie  (I passed for white)  I was framed

I was a burlesque queen, I was a teenage zombie
I was an adventuress, I was a convict, I was a criminal
I did it, I killed that man, murder is my beat, I confess

—for David Trinidad

into every life some possible lover should come.    you dor
you met him at the antelope petting zoo.    or on the steps o
some furry and with horns, some able.    some glistering in sv
some unable to stand erect, their soft boyparts pressed against

all the untouchable figures outspread upon the asphalt, as if
glowing snuff-colored against the motel background of a por
among the twenty-three airbrushed faces, slightly withdrawn, c

isn't he the one who looked upward into your gawp as if a dɛ
and the vessel protruded, your hull dragging up onto the bɛ
a feral thing, but he struck you, he bit you, and you broke insid

# Chronic

❧

# chronic

were lifted over the valley, its steepling dustdevils
the redwinged blackbirds convened
vibrant arc their swift, their dive against the filmy, the finite air

the profession of absence, of being absented, a lifting skyward
then gone
the moment of flight:  another resignation from the sweep of earth

jackrabbit, swallowtail, harlequin duck:  believe in this refuge
vivid tips of oleander
white and red perimeters where no perimeter should be


        here is another in my long list of asides:
why have I never had a clock that actually gained time?
that apparatus, which measures out the minutes, is our own image
                forever losing

and so the delicate, unfixed condition of love, the treacherous body
the unsettling state of creation and how we have damaged—
isn't one a suitable lens through which to see another:
        filter the body, filter the mind, filter the resilient land


and by *resilient* I mean *which holds*
        which tolerates the inconstant lover, the pitiful treatment
the experiment, the untried & untrue, the last stab at wellness

choose your own adventure:  drug failure or organ failure
cataclysmic climate change
or something akin to what's killing bees—colony collapse

more like us than we'd allow, this wondrous swatch of rough


why do I need to say the toads and moor and clouds—
in a spring of misunderstanding, I took the cricket's sound

and delight I took in the sex of every season, the tumble on moss
the loud company of musicians, the shy young bookseller
anonymous voices that beckoned to ramble
        to be picked from the crepuscule at the forest's edge

until the nocturnal animals crept forth
        their eyes like the lamps in store windows
            forgotten, vaguely firing a desire for home

hence, the body's burden, its resolute campaign:  trudge on

and if the war does not shake us from our quietude, nothing will

I carry the same baffled heart I have always carried
         a bit more battered than before, a bit less joy
for I see the difficult charge of living in this declining sphere


by the open air, I swore out my list of pleasures:
sprig of lilac, scent of pine
the sparrows bathing in the drainage ditch, their song

the lusty thoughts in spring as the yellow violets bloom
         and the cherry forms its first full buds
the tonic cords along the legs and arms of youth
         and youth passing into maturity, ripening its flesh
growing softer, less unattainable, ruddy and spotted plum


daily, I mistake—there was a medication I forgot to take
there was a man who gave himself, decently, to me & I refused him

in a protracted stillness, I saw that heron I didn't wish to disturb
was clearly a white sack caught in the redbud's limbs

I did not comprehend desire as a deadly force until—
      daylight, don't leave me now, I haven't done with you—
            nor that, in this late hour, we still cannot make peace


if I, inconsequential being that I am, forsake all others
how many others correspondingly forsake this world


     light, light:  do not go
I sing you this song and I will sing another as well

# Terminal C

# callas lover

this is the track I've had on REPEAT all afternoon:  she is butterfly
brilliant riband, rice flour face, silken, even her voice a sashed kimono

       if I were foolish like her:
              but aren't I foolish like her
          spotting the coil of smoke and the billowed sail
   against the verge of sky

simple on the rise surveying the anchorage:  simple me, signal me
dreading the confident assumption of return, dreading more
uncertain tone to come, the thinning notes, performance
too close to my own impatient—swells, a surge:  sick wind

but the emotion is, after all, an artfully conjured gesture
arranged marriage between a past ache and frail woodwinds
          I could skip ahead
               could break the inconsolable loop
of harbor, waiting, overlook, waiting, inevitable waning eye

troubled robins, once more in the handkerchief trees
once more, brief aquarelle of triplet lilies, blue as willowware
in that interval before his embrace falters, stuck, founders
       [shuffle play]    such a pitch of tenderness in the voice
         such an awful lot of noise

# coal of this unquickened world

midnight slips obsidian:  an arrowhead in my hand
pointed roofs against the backdrop, black and blacker
three kinds of ink, each more india than the last

must be going blind:  eyes two pitted olives on a cracker
a draught of the bitter ale, a kind of saturated past
poppy seeds:  black holes large as my head.   my head

dirty as a dishrag, crudely drawn imp, a charcoaled dove
disappearing down alleys with a pail from the chimney
this carbon:  no graphite nor diamond it's ordinary soot

dress it up:  say "buckminsterfullerene" or carbon$_{60}$
but it's just common, the color of a boot
a slate on the ground.   a petroleum bubble above

smothering in the walrus suit, the cloud of smoke
the shroud and deathmask.   blitzkrieg black sun choke

# shut the fuck up and drink your gin & tonic

all afternoon the mowers have been mowing:  watery eyes exhaust
this distorted tune: *smells like teen spunk*    the subwoofer thumps
coronary of another tragic neo-post-adolescent tooling up the street

to wind the engines of this oily-complected land: *yo-yo.*    walk the dog
around the world & bloody your upper lip  [the latter:  no regulation trick]
if there's one thread to be followed, it's "take your lumps and get your stitches"

send down the little nibblies, will you barkeep:  the ones called stupor
and deficit and "well, anyway, the cockroaches will survive."    oh, you kids:
still that awkward growth spurt that started when you were sperm

what bulges in your britches, besides your comb and a little manhood?
get yourself a pistol, if that's what it takes:  better than pulling up pathic knees
straddled by winking lawyers, butchers, fakers, cabinet-makers

listen, have you noticed the evening star gets a little lighter every night?
a bullseye spreads across your face:  you brittle bismuth:  how high the flame
burning pages, smudged headlines and ordinary terror alerts  [drive hertz!]

nobody said the undertaker would come spanking new in a blinding heat
his crucible searing arctic glaciers [indeed: *summer surprised us*]  kindling dry woodlands
damming brooks and poisoning this rank firmament:  he was a smiling devil, you know

the man who gives you congress, making a motion like a motion to suppress:  he's got you
amputated from the mind up:  tonight's entertainment: *everybody gets shtupped in the tokhes*
by the wry fellow who says "kiss me, I got keys to the pharmacy"  see?   [si, si, si]

—Apathy at Harvard, 2001–2004

## city upon a hill

the shape of landmass deviates its former line
chisel and saw the slope:  redraw the boundary
                where sea meets shore

        from the vantage out on the horizon:
a land made close, that we might navigate toward
the sheer incline of it, that we might cross that sea
                & raise a beacon upon that hill
                        to those who came, & after


previous to flight—and piles driven into bedrock
and, in no particular order:  girders, gasoline, pipeline
                the state:  the last cold climate
                        liquefaction of the arctic sheet—

there was a city beheld the waters exceeding its port
                and longed to traverse that profound body

"wide was the sea and far" embarks the city record

        the wind and wrack of pounding sea

                the dense, unmoving sea

# republic

soon, industry and agriculture converged
                and the combustion engine
sowed the dirtclod truck farms green
                   with onion tops and chicory

mowed the hay, fed the swine and mutton
             through belts and chutes

cleared the blue oak and the chaparral
                 chipping the wood for mulch

back-filled the marshes
             replacing buckbean with dent corn

removed the unsavory foliage of quag
                   made the land into a production
made it *produce*, pistoned and oiled
             and forged against its own nature

and—with enterprise—built silos
                   stockyards, warehouses, processing plants
abattoirs, walk-in refrigerators, canneries, mills
                  &centers of distribution

it meant something—in spite of machinery—
            to say *the country*, to say *apple season*
though what it meant was a kind of nose-thumbing
                 and a kind of sweetness
        as when one says *how quaint*
knowing that a refined listener understands the doubleness

and the leveling of the land, enduing it in sameness, cured malaria
as the standing water in low glades disappeared,
                                    as the muskegs drained

typhoid and yellow fever decreased
                        even milksickness abated
thanks to the rise of the feeding pen
                    cattle no longer grazing on white snakeroot

vanquished:  the germs that bedeviled the rural areas
                            the rural areas also
vanquished:  made monochromatic and mechanized, made suburban



now, the illnesses we contract are chronic illnesses:  dyspepsia, arthritis
            heart disease, kidney disease, high blood pressure, asthma
                    chronic pain, allergies, anxiety, emphysema
                            diabetes, cirrhosis, lyme disease, aids
            chronic fatigue syndrome, malnutrition, morbid obesity
hypertension, cancers of the various kinds:  bladder bone eye lymph
                    mouth ovary thyroid liver colon bileduct lung
                        breast throat & sundry areas of the brain

no better at accounting for death, and no worse:  we still die
we carry our uninhabited mortal frames back to the land
                    cover them in sod, we take the land to the brink
            of our dying:  it stands watch, dutifully, artfully
enriched with sewer sludge and urea
                                    to green against eternity of green

hocus-pocus:  here is a pig in a farrowing crate
                          eating its own feces
human in its ability to litter inside a cage
                  to nest, to grow gravid and to throw its young

I know I should be mindful of dangerous analogy:
          the pig is only the pig
                    and we aren't merely the wide-open field
                              flattened to a space resembling nothing


you want me to tell you the marvels of invention?    that we persevere
that the time of flourishing is at hand?    I should like to think it

meanwhile, where have I put the notebook on which I was scribbling

it began like:
                  "the smell of droppings and that narrow country road . . ."

# democrac

does god discriminate, slashing some flags, amendments

ever farther above the chapels, pale heaven expires

*mortar the mosque* means *build* not *bomb*—the moral center gives

only an honest fellow [please provide] might renounce

christ, this machinery of helmets, prosthetic limbs, human skin

refusing, louder than the drone above the disputed zones

all ages are difficult ages:  flight, the bits of metal raining down

clarity never arrives, it is a spar in a far mine, it cost us dearly

# untimely ripped of plastic

let's say the shiny exterior was the first thing to catch my fancy
his luxurious laminated curve, his tapering candle dripping wax
the hint of the forbidden that flickered there in the shadows

let's say caught evening pleated lines against the darkness
a grind and explosion: flak flak on the clean sofa, and fluid

sponge, suds.   the droplet leaking, snailsheen, licked icecream
the seawall gave, outward, it was an outward breaking

as if the cell of the brig had been breached, prisoners running
knowing they would be beaten mercilessly if caught, let's say

the figures, all of them manufactured in the mind's foreplay factory
had nothing to do with the difficult, hesitating contact, the first foray
an exploratory touch, a finger, a set of fingers pulling the snap

open: intervening fumble and tear, polythene package, stretch
but the partaken slipped sans capsheaf, nothing ribbed, spontaneous

arch, slip, and gleam, and let's just say dissent was squelched
carriers sailed in the gulf, banners, banners against the keel

# plague year: comet: arc

down came the irresistible, ghastly HE: beclouded cheval glass
the ugly visitation when the hearse pulls up to the curb
unmaking the night.  bugs.  the disarray of astonished bodies
hurling through the streets, between buildings broken
into myriad electrons, stitch of illuminated roofs the everlasting

HE: my bedfellow, my taint, the angel as expected
                    forsaking as expected, the apprehended angel
                          the funerary angel, the way HE fucks
                    like a bodybag, already empty, already depositing
              its contents atop the toxic landfill, giving up the corpus

giving up the skin and the assembly, giving up as expected
leaf and tree and blade, the verdure taken up
              stone and monument stone, instead, the concrete
                    and the crude pigiron hammered into steel

lightless HE.  unmerciful HE.  sad lamb HE: under the streetlamp
              proffering his expendable sex to expendable passers-by
                    forgive us this flesh, the way it presses to be admitted
              forgive this disheveled drapery of night:  pull back, pull back

# for the coming pandemic

bootless prayer.    his tongue swoll up, godspeed our sleeper
*siss* goes the air through his slackening cheeks

another degenerating, a third ashen, another yielding, of a sudden:
                    *good sir, I let you ravish me with your meaty hands—*
*throw down your crummy bag of tricks*, he mumbles in this manner
if he mumbles at all:  delirium:  parlance of stinging nettles

and now the speaker [who cannot speak] is a concert of voices
squelched, put down in the roads between shanties, put down
on paltry stretchers in corrugated tin towns, makeshift clinics

lands divided into plats.    the tenants put out beyond the gates

and in the midst of crowds, and under every eave and entryway
one hears the addled noise from occluded windpipes
and the sucking tongues cleaved to the ceilings in parched mouths

and the palaces are not saved, either, though they are palaces
and even the hospitals in fine neighborhoods are inundated

from above:  diving beaks and birdclaws, drawn by the scent
and lush carnation of the vivid sores:  the meatbees, too
gathering to the great banquet of humankind.
                                                            to the tender child:
take our tranquilizer.    take our anti-nausea, our generic
course of treatment, nutritional supplement, take
this little bit of water for your thirst, purified

the stream of your infancy diverted, treated, was never
the stream and its waterfowl, alighting:
> *gurgle* goes saliva threading the trachea

godspeed to the pinworms and the moldspores, godspeed
to nimble fingers that sew this fine new suit of clothes

# hepatitis ABC

when the nightnurse appears in your doorway
she's a raptor outlined by the last good light

she delivers tasteless reading matter, bland food
she brings the familiar clipboard.    she jots a note

a bird circles even as we speak, the ceiling leaks

already the lazy coroner has written his autopsy
based on labcoat observations.    sedated mice
their blackberry-colored incisions stapled shut


you are not being treated.    on the chart, your vitals
rise and tumble, rise and fall.    the transplant list

on which your name appears and crosses out

cross the riffle, cross the *t* and the final *t* in *patient*
          (in *unresponsive patient*)
you go slack in that dismal wing

                    —for Jane Flood

# cancer inside a little sea

for the rivers, draining toward the coast, carry such silt
and the red mangrove, entwining root with excrescent root
prospers its mighty nation—bubbleshell, jingleshell, rotting chips

the flecks of understory leaves, crud and algae, scum—
like a submerged derrick, its network of cables impenetrable
and profuse, the trees knot and twist, trap the water's swill

a ratsnake in the branches, girding the lowest bough
and the strangler fig constricting trunk to trunk, arterial mass
wrapped over, in the insidious embrace of virginia creeper

what has been garnered of this wetland except the twigs
organic and inorganic mud, quartz-rich and mercury-laden
the accumulation of contaminants, cadmium, diquat, toxaphene

and always, the sandbars eroding at the periphery
where freshwater meets saltwater, and sawgrass swamp
drains into estuaries and bay.   and always the balance

upset, as herbicides eradicate cat's claw vine
which has choked out carrotwood, which has displaced cypress
and the sea absorbs the toxins and eliminated matter

what does it matter now, what is self, what is I, who gets to speak
or who does not speak, whether the poems get written
whether the reader receives them whole, in part or not at all


child to come, what will you make of this scratched paradise
this receptacle of soil, water, seed, bee, floating scat and spore
brutal wind and brutal tide.    the insignificance of fortunes

## *he's a maniac, maniac*

in the stanley kubrick movie of your life, you are an isolated man
going slowly mad in the drunken pillory of the snow

chasing a little version of your self with an axe
because that's what every hour is doing:  chasing you

vexing, isn't it, how often you've tried to write your story
but the apparitions won't let you, and the bottle calls

from the ballroom, whispers of every dead season
at the overlook hotel.   it seems you've played this role before

why can't you just have closure?     it's a horror movie, stupid
the villain returns:  you are the villain:  any second last thoughts

# crossing into canaan

*Then there came again and touched me one like the appearance of a man,*
*and he strengthened me,*
—Daniel 10:18

febrile body I woke into:  nightsweats, stink of the toil of living:

where hands could not bear to approach me, the young man fingered

lay upon me, was himself a cool sponge, drew my perspiration to his lips
icechips held in his teeth, he pushed small bergs into my mouth

caressed the skeletal arms I've hidden in long sleeves
kissed neck and chest, belly rotten with pudgy organs, thickset flesh

he pressed against me, cock on cock and tongue against tongue
saw himself reflected in my marshy eyes and did not flinch such weakness

sustained by this capable stroke, boatswain of my crossing

I take the death I'm moored to, announced as a measureless promontory
and bob in the river as a bloated corpse, blue lips, vacant gaze

let the water fill my lungs until they rip their festive piñatas

because the one who comes to gather me, capricious angel
has that voice:    that voice that affirms me rising when this fever abates

## bound isaac

late the hour he came to me, a failing

& had nobody, assumed I would have nobody
now & forever amen

he was an agreeable boy straight-toothed, fair
a glinting countenance

as the waiting had been a test
as the clarity of irrefutable heaven had been withheld

& had nobody arrived in those last months
this little pinch of salt and this cold dwelling were all

then the charge of my soul would be lost
and my voice, too, pass into dust
and I would say:  great is the dust
take me into the dark, into the dark and lovely void

having no fortune to wager, I'd wager

then, given the increase—

then, given the seed and limb—

what demand it were to accept such intimacy

the worse to waive

chest of bronze, the lift and fall of his likeness
his lips his uncovered loins


the incense of newly-turned fields was everywhere
the dew upon recent blades

and I perceived the god of abandon

tense in the space between his passive body—
his body—and the boundless reach

## courthouse steps

to say no more of art than that it makes, by its very distraction
       a mode of abiding

accordingly, its variations:  each type of thread-and-piecework
       named *double engagement ring, log cabin*, or *broken dishes*
all built on the same geometric figures—
       precise interception of angle and line

so too each tale of love is rooted in that first tale:  the poet
       descending to the underworld
       finally granted his shade, who'll follow him
only to disappear again.    perhaps one version has them reunite
       affixed in their solo chromospheres the stars, which,
       to the human eye, appear to overlap

substanceless love
       immune at last to gravity and time—

in texas (I might as well recount this as a story) there's a town
       with a courthouse built on concrete and twisted iron
edified in red granite, capitals & architrave of red sandstone

with point and punch, a carver broached the effigy of his muse
he rendered her attractive features, down to the very blush

*of course* she spurned him,
*of course* there was another to whom she turned

love should not be written in stone but written in water
(I paraphrase the latin of catullus)


the sculptor carried on:  not just the face of his beloved
but the face of her other lover:
snaggle-toothed, wart-peppered, pudgy
them both, made into ugly caricatures of themselves, as wanton
as the carver perceived them, and as lewd


well, craze and degenerate and crack:  the portraits hold
though, long since, the participants have dwindled into dirt

beautiful.   unbeautiful.   each with an aspect of exactness


tread light upon this pedestal.   dream instead of a time before
your love disfigured, a time
withstanding even crass, wind-beaten time itself

# chia pet cemetery

the plot has been overgrown since the last good rain

visited fractured pottery to the grave

just the size of a posthole will do:  *le petit mort*

if there is a sheet of fog, it is a fleece, it is a circling flock
the night comes as a flag of crepe waving us down

*down fills the finest pillow*, you said, wiseacre

*wiseacre*, I said, because I didn't yet know its root

you said you'd take care of everything, as if
the very wish to be an umbrella could expand

first:  you need a good haircut and a shave

second:  what were we going to tend if not ourselves
not children.   adopt-a-highway.    a home for wayward beagles
water the plants, I said, water the damned plants
well, you did manage to water the plants

collapse :


thus the pit, the excavated *butt cleat*—
a mining term, yet terribly fitting
as *creep* [the slow movement downhill
        of bits of loose rock, unimpeded soil
            the eroding elements of the planet's core]

you said you were giving, and you gave
            the gob, the goaf, the dross of earth
loose coal, loose ore, fool's gold

the layer of rock called *parting*
                running through a seam of anthracite
fault zone:  where the angular fragments of stone
            cave and fracture and shear

you slag pile you:  terrestrial heave
                bottomed your way to the top

# crab louse

all the armor plates cannot protect you, eremite

the way you burrow into the vulnerable part of the forest
and pray god the clippers don't get you:  their blades
whirring above your chitinous form
threatening to whack your tiny head off at the thorax

you have clung to one liana after another
tarzan-swinging into each savory tuck and fold
of the map.    incautious the people who ran naked
in the dense light & let you—
                    [*people* meaning *me*.    & many others]

so the infestation starts:  one unguarded prick
a nook in which you suck and suck
until the itch to kill you, a primate reflex, prevails

as you gorge in the troughs and ditches of desire
plumping like an old man pickled in alcohol
the agile fingers seek you out, pull at your hind legs
crack your meaty shell, you token of fleeting devotion

a pest, a pest, a rubious skin:  douse us with kerosene

## congregation in glory

gibber the portal, you waggle sly & avert your eye
hither draws near thy master, that interval of release

as you press against the partition, into anyone, could be anyone
cunning as serpent:  how you extend and make your petition
flies unbuttoning and spreading their dove-grey flaps

your penchant for scrape of unknown teeth and fingered anus
too long denied you, denied in turn by the bride you took
for jaw and beer, the good wishes of decrepit parents
who want you happy, husbanded, not dallying in company

of strangers.    unction delivers in constellations upon you
fire of pentecost:  frothy sparge of asteroids:  you proceed
and the planets proceed and the canopy deepens its blue

surreptitious the night you travel in, casual contagion
babbling the one you seek adjacent and risen in his stall

# confidence man

midway charmer, indiscriminately flexed his smile
        a mask of liquor, the rowdy cowpoke
though his spangles came from a vintage shop
        and *rough times* meant *beach house*
and *beach house* meant *trust fund*.   and *trust*
        meant — let us say *shameless*, to be kind

do you wish to doodle for a while on his photo?
        draw horns, then, where there ought to be horns
and a heart where there should have been a heart
        a bigger blank where definitely there was a blank

were you a sucker?   sure:  planchette of the ouija board
        unsubtle pads of his hands steered your head
into spaces marked YES and YES and, one time
        made you spell out MY NAME IS SAMUEL RIZZO
or something like that.   frankly wasn't it all a little garbled
        that western-style belt got in the way
its buckle, like an inconvenient tombstone, scraped at your nose

        when you opened the casket inside his earthy mound
he stood as the momentary resurrection of a childhood friend
        who might have been called billy, who might
have suffocated, cyanotic in his turtleneck, one-gallon hat

        who might have staged his own death, might have
plotted yours.   in the hayloft in the barn —
        why not allow that at least the setting was genuine?
for history is imprecise and all buildings fall to ruin —
        he laid out his hokum, he laid out his bunk

on his back, on his belly, cheap accordion of his buttocks
        faux-pearl buttons chipping as they hit the floor
the stink of his rucksack, ruined by rain, the stink
        of his unwashed scrotum, the dry slit of his knob
the driblets, the abdicated parts, the thing he slid into you
        the pinky, the prod, the extension of him
the boodle, the wad, the carnival ride with the broken gear

        you know how it is when you're sick, disoriented:
too many corndogs, funnel cakes, sideshows, come-ons

        step right up, it's frontierland, it's the wild wild west
three-card monte, one-eyed jack:  throw down your dollar
        my lucky friend:  follow, my boy, my lucky lucky boy

# barbershop talc

the only place left to shave is inside your ears
you are almost perfectly smooth:  the way you lie
the way you lift your rump like a powdery teacake

you are a gelid centerpiece at your best friend's wedding
you are an iceprincess of a man, frozen in time
everything you do, you do in time:  you arrive in time
you depart in time, but you never save yourself in time
that's the one thing you can't do:  save yourself

and so you shave yourself instead:  back of the neck
chest, nipples, balls.    the strop struck with the blade
cries the same desperate tone that the soapmug employs
it's a whisking sound, it's a gooey sound
you serve yourself like a creamy dessert
smooth, remarkably smooth, somebody should cut you
again, dust you and serve you to the bride's stupid sister
stupid enough to believe you as sugar, counterfeit groom

*cruel, cruel summer*


either the postagestamp-bright inflorescence of wild mustard
or the drab tassel of prairie smoke, waving its dirty garments

either the low breeze through the cracked window
or houseflies and drawn blinds to spare us the calid sun

one day commands the next to lie down, to scatter:  we're done
with allegiance, devotion, the malicious idea of what's eternal

picture the terrain sunk, return of the inland sea, your spectacle
your metaphor, the scope of this twiggy dominion pulled under

crest and crest, wave and cloud, the thunder blast and burst of swells
this is the sum of us:  brief sneezeweed, brief yellow blaze put out

so little, your departure, one plunk upon the earth's surface,
one drop to bind the dust, a little mud, a field of mud

the swale gradually submerged, gradually forgotten
and that is all that is to be borne of your empirical trope:

first, a congregated light, the brilliance of a meadowland in bloom
and then the image must fail, as we must fail, as we

graceless creatures that we are, unmake and befoul our beds
don't tell me *deluge.*    don't tell me *heat, too damned much heat*

# chrysanthemum

wherever he wakes this morning, he knows the big bang is irreparable

the following appraisal of saturn's rings:  water, electrically charged particles
        specks of obliterated satellites & largely unoccupied dark bands—
yes, they seem beautiful from this distance, as do so many colliding forms

        on the newsfeed, rockets spray across the lacquered box often
& often, in a world which is now so completely occupied
        a freighter spills its tenebrous rings into the overburdened bay

maybe he's eyeing his own depleted sac, remembering the lumps of jellyfish
        littering the shore with their baggy lappets and plasticine bells
maybe remembering carries no import now, since—space:  relativity
        roseate sunset, the way the rays refract through the pollution

the rays remind him of the little jellies on the beach, tentacles splayed

with a certain tilt of the mind, an imperial flower might mean forgiveness
        & might even the most remote explosion be read as a sign of triumph

## *cock* **on the radio**

is avian, this moderator with the microphone, birdlike
in that she hops about, skittish and pasty, the cockatoo
treading her perch with a nervous eye, neckfeathers puffed
and clutching the mike like a last cuttlebone, *fear you*
language, *fear you*, silence, squawks and her eye
in convulsive blink: *I hear you. scandalous. thinking*

peck.   the wild eye of the bird evaporating its pupil
a frightened version of the salton sea, crusted edge
where the snail bodies crunch underfoot.   *oh, I hear it*
the split tongue rehearses its mock surprise *I hear*

fury overhead, the hoo-ha striking the air a furious blow
no sound:  if it is a seed, she catches it in her craw
cranes her awk neck to dislodge the offending particle
shakes winglice, nits, a flit, a flit.   showering scurf upon
you. sordid. listen.   queer the pleasure of her vaudeville hook

—for Jeff Nagy and Eleanor Boudreau

## clown burial in winter

meringue icing beaten over hot water, ruffle-edged
and the occasional rosette atop an otherwise vanilla
sheet cake boxed in paraffined cardboard, raffia-tied:

maybe we can squint the midget into pastry, instead
of the polymer resin rectangular planter, impervious
to drought (unlike its plumes of maiden grass, gone dead

despite the youthful fuzz and tolerance to neglect)
that's one way to abide the loss.   or change the japer
to a swan:  pallid jewel set in the mind's frozen lake

just long enough to dip its beak—sheepstorm imminent,
cloudbank chattering diminished pinhead chatter    —
what madness drew this little man's painted grimace:

down-turned mouth on whiteface.   his droopy drawers
canvas the landscape.    a band of tin whistles plays
*pop the balloons*. it's a fine serenade.    burst of applause

# scenes from the trip we didn't take to the antarctic

your inability to phone says it all:  whitecaps frozen in a touchless curl
the space in the lungs where breath catches and falters

portage across the blank surface of the hills, bleached tendons
and the stark crevasse we could not cross:  we came to that impasse

laden with the starkest gear and most meager provisions
the landscape offered its monotonous signboard disproof

gentle soul, I can tell you now, there's no real continent underneath
the bluffs thin their beards and the glaciers chuckle to pea gravel

static the air, conclamant stars sheen the black sky, fisheye stilled
and time comes grinding to rest against the freezing waste of us

caught in an icy mortality:  we found its echo in eco tourism

you think an *ever* can change the course of vanishing
conjugate the verb any way you wish, you still lack future tense

say it with me, sunshine:  today, brainscan; today, x-ray
today, complete metabolic panel with platelet differential
today, urinalysis; today, liver biopsy; today, preparing the body

at the last station, the sepulcher was empty and you asked why
beyond this numbing terrain, frozen white cell:  phantom laughter
didn't you hear it all along?    or did you think it was just the wind

## corydon & alexis

shepherdboy?   not the most salient image for contemporary readers
nor most available.   unless you're thinking BROKEBACK MOUNTAIN:
a reference already escaping.   I did love a montana man, though no good shepherd

rather:  a caveman, came spelunking into that grotto I'd retreated to

what light he bore illumined such small space—physically, temporally

*and did he have a grove of beech trees?*   no, no grove
but together we found an old-growth stand of redwood

we gouged each other's chests instead of wood:  pledges that faded
he was not cruel nor I unwitting.   but what endures beyond any thicket?

example:  he took me to the ocean to say farewell.   I mean me:  farewell to ocean
the ocean, for that matter, to me.   us both fatigued, showing signs of wreckage

and that man I had loved stood back from the edge of things

he did not hold me

I expected not to be held

we all understood one another:  shepherd understudy, ocean, me

*and did he go back to his fields and caves?*   yes, but they were gone
strip-mining, lumber, defoliant, sterile streams:  you *knew* that was coming

weren't we taught some starched sermon:  the pasture awaits us elsewhere


*back up a moment:  the forest you mentioned—remember, instead of a grove?*

untouched for the most part.   some human damage, but not ours
we left no mark, not there in the midst of those great trees:
not in the concentric rings that might have held us far past living

instead, I put that man, like so many others, on paper—
a tree already gone from sight where once it had drawn the eyes
upward:  the crest of a mountain.   crumpled thoughts, crumpled love


shepherdboy, do you see the wild fennel bulbs I gathered for you
olallieberries, new-mown grass, the tender fruits of the coastal fig?

I put them on paper, too, so fragile.   for nothing is ever going to last

## corydon & alexis, redux

and yet we think that song outlasts us all:  wrecked devotion
the wept face of desire, a kind of savage caring that reseeds itself and grows in clusters

oh, you who are young, consider how quickly the body deranges itself
how time, the cruel banker, forecloses us to snowdrifts white as god's own ribs


what else but to linger in the slight shade of those sapling branches
yearning for that vernal beau.    for don't birds covet the seeds of the honey locust
and doesn't the ewe have a nose for wet filaree and slender oats foraged in the meadow
kit foxes crave the blacktailed hare:  how this longing grabs me by the nape


guess I figured to be done with desire, if I could write it out
dispense with any evidence, the way one burns a pile of twigs and brush

*what was his name?* I'd ask myself, that guy with the sideburns and charming smile
the one I hoped that, as from a sip of hemlock, I'd expire with him on my tongue


silly poet, silly man:  thought I could master nature like a misguided preacher
as if banishing love is a fix.    as if the stars go out when we shut our sleepy eyes

# Acknowledgments

Some of these poems first appeared in the following journals: *Absomaly, A Gathering of the Tribes, Alaska Quarterly Review, American Letters & Commentary, Black Warrior Review, Boston Review, Boulevard, Cincinnati Review, Colorado Review, Columbia Journal, Conduit, Court Green, Cutbank, Denver Quarterly, dritto, Electronic Poetry Review, Eucalyptus, Gulf Coast, Jacket,* the *Kenyon Review, linebreak.org, Margie, New England Review, New Orleans Review, Octopus, Other Than, Pebble Lake Review, Pistola, Pleiades, Poetry, Quarterly West, Smartish Pace, Subtropics,* the *Pinch, Tin House, Virginia Quarterly Review, Volt,* and *Zoland Poetry.*

"coit tower & us" appeared as a limited edition broadside, designed by Roni Gross and printed by the Center for Book Arts in New York, New York.

"corydon and alexis, redux" was adapted and set to music by Jascha Hoffman. It debuted on 12 October, 2006, in his *The Dream Show.*

"sprig of lilac" was reprinted from *Pleiades* on the website *Poetry Daily.*

"callas lover" appeared in *Poetry Calendar 2009* (Alhambra Publishing, Belgium, 2008).

"california poppy" "crematorium at sierra view cemetery, next to the high school" and "clutch and pumps" appeared in the anthology *American Hybrid* (Norton, 2008).

"lipsync [with a nod to lipps, inc.]" appeared in *Satellite Convulsions: Poems from Tin House* (Tin House Books, 2008).

"cosmos, late blooming" appeared in the anthology *Best American Poetry 2008* (Scribner, 2008), edited by Charles Wright.

"central valley" appeared in the anthology *Something Understood: Essays and Poetry for Helen Vendler* (University of Virginia Press, 2009).

Thanks to the Millay Colony for the Arts, for a residency that allowed me time to finish writing this book.

Thanks to University of San Francisco, Dean Jennifer Turpin and Assistant Deans Peter Novak and Dean Rader for faculty development funds and sabbatical time, crucial to the writing of this book.

And thanks to those who read and responded to portions of this manuscript while it was in process: Jeff Shotts, Kate Brady and Steve Kahn, Carol Ciavonne, Ryan Courtwright, Rob Dennis, Sarah Estes, Luke Goebels, Jorie Graham, Kristen Hanlon and John Isles, Jascha Hoffman, Rachel Loden, Jeff Nagy, Timothy O'Keefe, Kevin Prufer, Susan Steinberg, Peter Streckfus, Mary Szybist, Brian Teare, Michael Theune, David Trinidad, Mary Wang, Sam Witt, Matthew Zapruder, Rachel Zucker, and my constant reader and friend J. Peter Moore.

D. A. Powell's previous collections are *Tea, Lunch,* and *Cocktails*. He teaches in the English Department of University of San Francisco.

This book was designed by Connie Kuhnz. It is set in Legacy Serif type by BookMobile Design and Publishing Services, Minneapolis, Minnesota, and manufactured by Sheridan Books on acid-free paper.